Usborne

Can we really HELP the Dolphins?

YES you can.

Katie Daynes

illustrated by Róisín Hahessy

designed by Helen Lee

It could be an important message.

Ah-hargh!

Maybe it's a cry for help from a shipwrecked pirate!

Or an invitation to a mermaid's party.

Dear Kids on Land,

Our home is in danger and we think YOU can help. We'll come to your pier to tell you more.

See you on the longest day of the year.

Yours gratefully,
Dolphin and Friends

The longest day...
that's TODAY!

Quick!
Let's go to the pier.

What's so bad about plastic?

IT **NEVER** ROTS AWAY.

Plastic litter builds up in the sea
and drifts even to the most faraway shores.

Sea creatures get tangled in it,
or swallow it by mistake.

Yikes!
Let me help.

Over time, plastic breaks
into smaller pieces, but it
DOESN'T disappear.

I can see lots
of tiny pieces
in the seawater.

They're called
microplastics.

But it's not just plastic that's bothering us. Humans make all kinds of things that POLLUTE the sea.

What does POLLUTE mean?

It means SPLURGING OUT dirty, harmful stuff, from oil and chemicals to toilet waste.

Toilet waste?
That's GROSS!

Imagine what it's like to swim in.

No thank you!

But the sea is our HOME and when it's not being spoiled by humans, it's an AMAZING place to live.

There are floating icy islands...

...and deep blue sea as far as the eye can see.

Animals of all shapes and sizes live here...

from tiny pink krill, to the biggest animals that ever lived...

...blue whales.

woooo ooo ooo

Seabirds dive to catch their dinner.

Small animals shelter in coral reef cities.

And shimmering schools of fish twist and turn and travel to new places.

It's so beautiful.

The
deeper
you
go,
the darker it gets
and the stranger
the creatures.

How BIG is the sea?

Arctic Ocean

Atlantic Ocean

Pacific Ocean

Indian Ocean

Southern Ocean

It's
ENORMOUS!

The world's seas and oceans all flow into each other, making one gigantic ocean.

It covers over 70% of the Earth's surface.

But our ocean is becoming really hard to live in.
That's why we need your help.

What can WE do?

We're not the ones POLLUTING your ocean.

We all live hundreds of miles from the sea.
We're only visiting for the summer.

And where do you think the fish you eat comes from?

The sea!

Yes!

Is eating fish a problem? I mean, there must be ZILLIONS of fish in the sea.

It wouldn't be a problem, if humans caught fish RESPONSIBLY.

But selling fish and other seafood is BIG BUSINESS. Fishing companies are using bigger ships and bigger nets and they're sifting more and more wildlife from the sea.

If this carries on, we'll **ALL** be in **BIG** trouble.

The ocean might RUN OUT of fish...

...and be filled with PLASTIC instead!

That would be TERRIBLE.

Did you know,
you're also connected
to the sea by the air
you breathe.

No way!

Yes way!

You need OXYGEN
from the air to LIVE...

...and over half the
world's oxygen
comes from the sea.

It bubbles up from
seaweed forests and
seagrass meadows.

Oxygen also bubbles out of tiny living things called PLANKTON.

Here are some plankton made 50 times bigger.

There are vast crowds of plankton drifting in the ocean's tides and currents.

How do plankton and other things make oxygen?

Funnily enough, oxygen is what they GET RID OF when they make their own food.

They take in WATER and a gas called CARBON DIOXIDE from the ocean...

CO_2

Yum yum!

...and use SUNLIGHT to turn them into a sugary food.

OXYGEN is what's left over.

O_2

It bubbles out for the rest of the planet to use.

Oxygen is O_2 for short, and carbon dioxide is CO_2.

Ooh, thanks plankton!

How does the carbon whatsit get INTO the ocean?

Carbon dioxide?

It dissolves into the seawater from the air.

CO_2 CO_2 CO_2 CO_2

CO_2

CO_2

CO_2

CO_2

CO_2

In fact, the seaweeds, seagrasses and plankton do a great job of taking in LOTS of the carbon dioxide made by humans.

CO_2 CO_2

CO_2

Whooooo

Oooh is that the gas we breathe out?

We can't help that!

Breathing out CO_2 is fine.
The problem comes when lots of
EXTRA CO_2 is added to the air.
It's made by burning coal, oil and gas...

CO_2 CO_2 CO_2 CO_2 CO_2

to power your vehicles...

your factories...

...and your homes.

CO_2 CO_2 CO_2 CO_2 CO_2 CO_2 CO_2

But MORE CO_2 should
make the plankton happy!

Not really.
There's a limit on how much
CO_2 the plankton can absorb.
Too much CO_2 makes the
water more ACIDIC.

Acidic?

Yes. Acids are sour
liquids, like lemon juice.
And acidic water isn't nice to live in.

It ruins
our shells.

Ours too.

We need our shells
to protect us.

It weakens
our coral reefs.

Yuck, too much acid.

It makes it
harder for our
babies to grow.

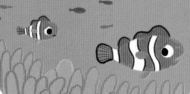

Ugh!

And it can also
harm those tiny
oxygen-makers,
plankton!

Oh no!

The main reason for climate change is TOO MUCH CO_2 in the air.

It traps the sun's heat, making our planet and its oceans **WARM UP** too much.

CO_2 CO_2 CO_2 CO_2 CO_2 CO_2 CO_2 CO_2 CO_2 CO_2 CO_2 CO_2 CO_2 CO_2 CO_2 CO_2 CO_2 CO_2 CO_2 CO_2 CO_2 CO_2 CO_2 CO_2

Oooh warmer water to swim in – that sounds nice.

It's not so nice for the animals and plants.

Even a small temperature change can mean we struggle to survive.

Polar animals need freezing cold weather or the ice melts and they can't hunt for food.

That's right!

And if snow and ice on the land melt too, the meltwater runs into the sea and makes the sea level rise.

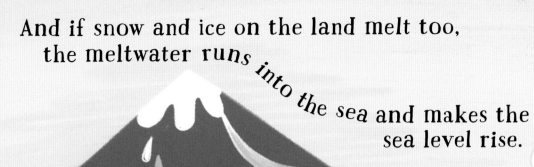

Water is already lapping up higher around islands and seaside towns.

Meanwhile, the air above is getting WILDER.

Moist, hot air rises quickly above the warm ocean and swirls around making huge, powerful storms.

We can't enjoy the beach if it's stormy or flooded.

Or polluted with yucky things.

And we don't want the sea creatures to die!

We must
PROTECT OUR SEAS AND OCEANS.

Let's STOP MAKING TOO
MUCH CARBON DIOXIDE.

And all the other kinds
of POLLUTION!

YES!

YES!

YES!

And let's STOP CATCHING
TOO MANY FISH.

YES!

YES!

YES!

Do we have to stop eating fish?

No, fish is good for you.

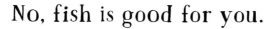

But gigantic nets are BAD because they catch **WHOLE SCHOOLS** of fish and put entire species in danger.

And heavy nets called bottom trawlers are bad too, because they scrape and ruin the ocean floor.

We must have caught a million today.

Oh no, they trap dolphins and turtles, too!

Why don't fishing companies use rods or smaller nets, so they don't take so many fish at once?

Some of us do!
And we throw back the fish we don't want, too.

YAY!

This makes fishing more SUSTAINABLE.

What does sustainable mean?

Not taking too many of the same kind of fish...

...so there will always be more in the future.

But how do we know if a fish company IS being sustainable?

Often there's a label on their packaging telling you.

CERTIFIED SUSTAINABLE SEAFOOD

Inspectors check up on the companies and only award labels to the sustainable ones.

Great. This packet is OK to buy.

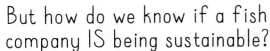

What about all the plastic filling up the sea?

Why don't people take their litter home with them?

Beats me!

And why are so many things made of plastic in the first place?

Because it's waterproof and tough, it can be made into all shapes and sizes, and it can last for ages.

But it's bonkers to make stuff we throw away out of something that lasts for AGES!

We know!

50 years and it's still here!

What about other pollution?

How do we stop yucky stuff like sewage from reaching the sea?

This tanker has run aground and the oil is spilling out.

Let's make a BIG FUSS about it. Tell the people in charge that it's RUINING our ocean, making people UNWELL and KILLING our sea creatures.

Chemicals from this farm are seeping straight into the river.

This harmful dye is leaking from a clothes factory.

The trickiest problem is how to stop climate change.

It seems TOO BIG and complicated for us to solve.

But it's quite simple really.

Burn LESS
coal
oil
gas

We just need to stop making extra CO_2. Then it can't trap in heat and warm up our planet!

Well when you put it like that...

There are BETTER ways to power our vehicles and homes.

Like the shining of the SUN!

The whizzing of the WIND!

The whooshing of WATER!

And our own muscle power!

Brilliant!
There's lots of wind power out at sea.

And you can use the power of the waves and the tides as well.

My dad is designing a container ship with sails. It runs on wind power instead of burning oil.
HOORAY!

Also, making less carbon dioxide means less acidy water.

And happier shellfish.

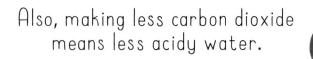

That's better!

Some divers recently found a happy, healthy coral reef that's deeper than the others.

Ooh, that's interesting.

We're happy because it's cooler down here.

We're all going to have to adapt a bit to cope with changes in the climate.

But if humans can stop the world from warming up TOO much...

...then climate change won't be so bad.

People are planting lots of trees on land to help SLOW DOWN climate change.

Can we do something like that in the water?

TREE PLANTING

YES!

You can plant things like seagrass meadows and mangrove swamps.

They trap carbon in their roots and make more oxygen.

And they protect coastlines from flooding too.

Let's mention this in the video.

I'm writing a TO DO list for the people in charge.

Great!

TO DO

* Clean up sewage
* Make laws on fishing
* Ban throwaway plastic
* Plant more seagrass

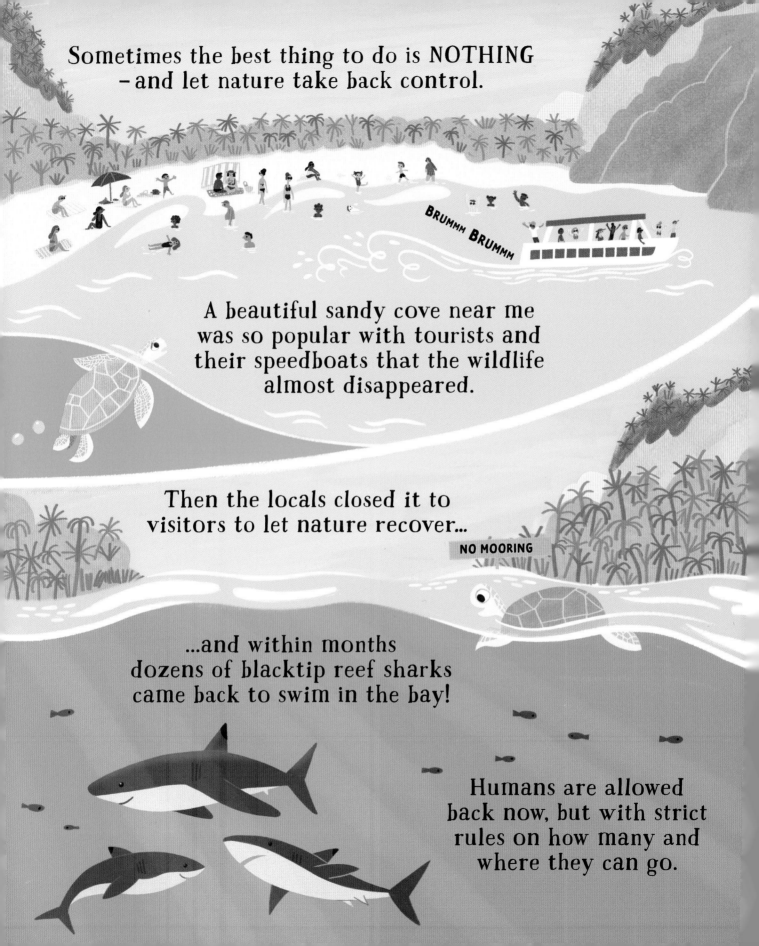

Sometimes the best thing to do is NOTHING – and let nature take back control.

BRUMMM BRUMMM

A beautiful sandy cove near me was so popular with tourists and their speedboats that the wildlife almost disappeared.

Then the locals closed it to visitors to let nature recover...

NO MOORING

...and within months dozens of blacktip reef sharks came back to swim in the bay!

Humans are allowed back now, but with strict rules on how many and where they can go.

I guess speedboats aren't great for nature.

Their propellors can damage the seabed.

And they're VERY NOISY.

I've got loads of great footage for a video now!

And I've made some notes to explain the more complicated things.

Let's see how we can put it together...

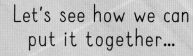

People are putting lots of yucky things into the sea...

...and taking out TOO many fish.

Sea creatures, plants and algae are in danger...

...and that's bad for us, too.

Climate change is a BIG PROBLEM.

But we can all be part of the solution.

The people in charge need to DO MORE.

Countries need to make strict LAWS and ENFORCE them.

We can ALL play our part by making ocean-friendly choices...

helping to RESTORE NATURE...

making less litter...

...and telling everyone about our AMAZING ocean.

Our schools might show
the video in assembly.

This was made by one
of our students.

OUR MOVIE
HELP the DOLPHINS

It could go VIRAL...

Have you seen this?!

...and inspire lots
of campaigners.

We all need the
OXYGEN plants make.

Plastic WON'T rot away.

BAN
throwaway
plastic

This shouldn't be allowed.

STOP SEWAGE
SPLURGES

Wow, what
a great idea.

SAVE THE DOLPHINS

Our government will have to sit up and take notice.

SEWAGE DISCHARGE

Oh dear, it's true.
Water companies have been discharging more raw sewage.

We must introduce stricter laws and fines.

THERE'S A SWIRLING SOUP OF PLASTIC IN THE OCEAN THAT'S **THREE TIMES** THE SIZE OF FRANCE

And countries around the world could agree to help the ocean.

The world NEEDS action!
Let's have a global treaty on STOPPING plastic pollution.

WORLD LEADERS' OCEAN MEETING

We'll sign it!

So will we.

And us!

Us too.

What next?

The problems the dolphins and their friends describe in this book are REAL and affect us ALL. But the GOOD NEWS is that things are already changing...

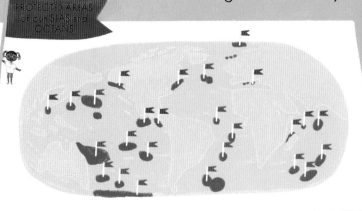

PROTECTED AREAS of our SEAS and OCEANS

Large parts of the ocean have become PROTECTED AREAS, with restrictions on shipping and fishing.

Thank you!

Governments responsible for 40% of the world's coastlines have promised to END OVERFISHING and help fish populations to recover.

Many countries have already BANNED single-use plastic items and are introducing a TAX on plastic packaging.

Areas equivalent to thousands of football fields have been successfully replanted with seagrass, and many more restoration projects are planned.

Thanks!

There's still LOTS MORE TO DO and we can all play a part in protecting our oceans.

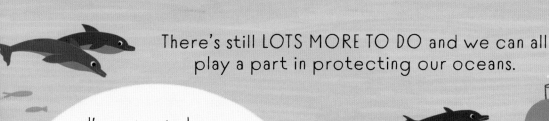

I'm going to be an INVENTOR and develop a natural alternative to plastic.

I'm going to be a MARINE BIOLOGIST and learn more about how we can protect dolphins.

I'm going to be a POLITICIAN and make laws stopping companies from causing pollution.

I'm going to start a CONSERVATION CHARITY, raising money to restore coastal areas.

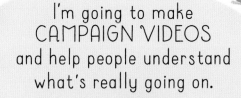

Coastal Conservation $1,000,000

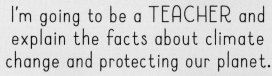

I'm going to make CAMPAIGN VIDEOS and help people understand what's really going on.

I'm going to be a TEACHER and explain the facts about climate change and protecting our planet.

Glossary

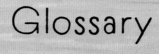

Here are some of the important words
in this book and what they mean.

acidic – sour or sharp-tasting.

carbon dioxide (CO_2) – one of the heat-trapping
gases people make when they burn oil, coal and gas.

chemicals – substances made using a scientific process.
There are chemicals in nature, but the ones causing
pollution in this book are made by people.

climate change – a change in weather patterns around
the world. Human activities are making the world get
warmer, and this is causing climate change.

coral reef – a large underwater structure made by
thousands of tiny animals called coral polyps.

discharge – letting out a waste liquid or gas.

mangrove – a type of tree that lives in salty water
along warm coastlines.

microplastics – very small pieces of plastic.
Plastic litter breaks up into microplastics.

oxygen – the gas we all need to breathe in to live.

overfishing – taking too many fish from the ocean,
so whole species start to die out.

plankton - very small living things that float in the sea.

pollution - harmful stuff that damages the planet.

sewage - liquid and solid waste from toilets.

species - a group of the same kind of living things.

sustainable - doing something in a way that means things won't run out in the future.

treaty - a written agreement between two or more countries, signed by their leaders.

Usborne Quicklinks

For links to websites where you can dive with dolphins, and find videos and activities about how we can help ocean animals, visit usborne.com/Quicklinks and type in the title of this book.

Please follow the internet safety guidelines at Usborne Quicklinks.

Children should be supervised online.

Edited by Jane Chisholm

Ocean expert: Jo Ruxton

With additional inspiration from
Zoe Wray and the dolphins

First published in 2023 by Usborne Publishing Limited, 83-85 Saffron Hill, London, EC1N 8RT. usborne.com